Dopam

Dopamine Decor

Sofia Meri

Published by LAURENT MERI, 2023.

DOPAMINE DECOR

First edition. September 4, 2023.

Written by Sofia Meri.

Table of Contents

Table of Contents

How To Make Your Home Decoration a Serotonin And Dopamine Agonist and Detox Your Body And Mind

By Sofia Meri

Wanna Hear a Little Secret? Keep It Short

In today's world of super-short attention spans, you gotta trim the fat if you want to pay attention to hot takes. Sure, jumbo books look impressive on your shelf. But when it comes to real talk, shorter is sweeter.

Short books give you a laser-focused highlight without all the boring backstory or fluff. Their every sentence packs a punch, not wasted words.

Got an earth-shattering idea? Don't bury it under 600 pages of dust-dry prose. Distil that sucker down to its purest, minimalist form. Like a perfectly blended smoothie, filter out the unnecessary chunks for maximum impact.

Besides, who has time for lengthy door topper tomes anymore? We want knowledge in bite-size nuggets now. With fit-for-purpose books, you can suck down those nourishing morsels in a few sittings, retaining way more. Really let the savoury flavours marinate.

And don't forget the sharing! Itty bitty ideas spread like hot fire because everyone has time for a quick but amazing story. Just ask that monk dude with the Ferrari - his cliff's notes wisdom went viral faster than a Kanye rant.

So do yourself a favour and keep it short. Chop off any unnecessary padding. Get straight to the good stuff and deliver it with gravitas.

Less is more when you choose each word with care.

Enhancing Your Reading with Complementary Visuals

―――

While this guide focuses on clearly articulating the philosophies, psychology, and foundational principles behind dopamine decorating through words, I recognize many readers also appreciate accompanying visual examples.

Pictures allow you to vividly envision how these uplifting design concepts might translate into tangible spaces, color palettes, arrangements, and motifs. You conceptualize more fully when absorbing principles both verbally and visually.

That's why I offer access to the Sofia Meri Interior Design Guide. This photo-rich online resource excellently demonstrates visual examples.

With vivid imagery of finished spaces, the guide allows you to illuminate this book in action.

Scan or follow the link below

rebrand.ly/SofiaMeri

WELCOME TO THE HAPPY home of your dreams! Within these pages, you'll find everything you need to surround yourself with uplifting décor that reflects your unique spirit.

This book is intended as a guide, not a rulebook. It contains tips and principles, not strict steps or required checklists. The goal is simply to help you gain clarity around your own decorating style and confidence in designing feel-good spaces that spark inspiration.

There's no need to read the chapters in order or apply every suggestion exactly as written. Feel free to skip around to the sections most appealing and relevant to your needs. Absorb what resonates, then adapt the concepts in ways that feel authentic to you.

Decorating should be an enjoyable process of self-discovery, not a stressful quest for perfection. Progress will happen organically over time through Trial and error as you learn more about your tastes and what environments lift you up. Give yourself permission to play, experiment and get creative without self-judgment.

You may want to keep this book handy for when you need a quick hit of inspiration before heading to a thrift store or making updates to your home. Refer back to the tips that stood out most and jot down additional ideas in the margins. Mark pages with Post-Its to easily refind beloved passages.

Most importantly, remember that you are the expert on designing happily inspiring spaces for yourself. Use the guidance in this book as a supportive starting point, then bravely build upon it to craft rooms as unique as your spirit. Surround yourself with pieces, colors, and styles that authentically resonate with your energy.

Now, let's begin exploring the principles of uplifting dopamine decor! Wishing you many delightful hours spent creating a cozy, colorful, creativity-sparking haven. May your home become a sacred space shining with the light of your one-of-a-kind essence. Let's do this!

Introduction : Dopamine Decor For A Happy Life

Welcome to the happy home of your dreams! With the turn of this page, you're taking the first step towards creating a living space that fully reflects the colorful, playful, and warm vibes of your unique personality. If the sea of sterile, all-white apartments and homes marked by mass-produced decor makes you yearn for something more vibrant and meaningful, you've come to the right place.

In this book, we'll explore the blithe spirit of dopamine decor - an interior design approach focused entirely on surrounding yourself with furniture, art, textiles, colors, and treasured keepsakes that spark joy deep within your soul. Unlike fleeting trends that come and go, dopamine decor is forever. Why? Because it's inherently based on you -your distinctive style, favorite aesthetics, and the nostalgic pieces that never fail to make you smile.

While some minimalist homes may boast sleek lines and tidy organization, they often lack the levity and heart that turns a house into a happy home. Through dopamine decorating, we inject lightness and life back into interior design, embracing playful patterns, radiant colors, time-honored family heirlooms, and tactile textures that beg to be touched. This signature style provides the perfect antidote to cookie-cutter rooms devoid of personality.

Within these pages, our goal is to help you curate spaces brimming with joy, energy, and nostalgia. You won't find strict rules here or pressure to conform to fleeting fads. Instead, through a series of fun exercises, prompts, and decor dilemmas, we'll explore your cherished memories, favorite aesthetics, and unique quirks to uncover design choices that authentically represent you.

While creating a beautifully personalized haven, we'll also discuss key principles of color theory, sourcing special finds, displaying memorabilia, and pulling rooms together seamlessly. You can start small with pops of sunny yellow pillows or go all-in by bathed your bedroom in your favorite hue from floor to ceiling. The beauty of dopamine decor is that it meets you wherever you're at in your design journey and grows as you do.

This book was created to help you follow your creative spirit without reservation or limitation. Within these pages, you have the encouragement and guidance needed to transform your home into a playful, energizing oasis where you can recharge and be wholly, authentically you. As you turn each page, remember that there are no rules in dopamine decor - only joy. Any choice that brings you happiness and nostalgic warmth belongs in your space.

Are you ready to immerse yourself in colors that lift your mood, prints that make you smile, and treasured finds filled with memories and meaning? Then let's get started designing your dreamiest, happiest home yet! Permission granted to have fun.

A Note Before We Begin...

———————

FIRST, THANK YOU SINCERELY for reading this book! My goal is to provide value and help you create a home environment that lifts your spirit.

If you find the advice in this guide useful for surrounding yourself with joyful décor, you'd be doing me a massive favor by taking a minute to leave an honest positive review on the platform where you purchased the book. Here's why it matters:

Positive word-of-mouth is crucial for books like this to spread and make an impact. Your review gives algorithms a signal that these dopamine decorating tips are helping people live happier lives.

That then allows me to reach and assist many more design enthusiasts just like you. My dream is improving wellbeing at scale by teaching people how to turn their homes into personal sanctuaries through purposeful décor.

But that can't happen without reviews from awesome readers. And you are an AWE...SOMe reader! So if this book resonates with you, please boost the signal with a positive review. It would mean the world to me and this community.

Shifting home décor habits isn't easy – we need all the inspiration we can get! With your small action, together we can share this uplifting message more widely and spark positive changes.

Plus, you'll likely inspire someone in your life who needs this book too. Paying it forward creates ripples.

Okay, sincerely thank you for even considering leaving your feedback. Now let's dive into these unbelievable décor upgrades!

Chapter 1: Understanding Dopamine Decor

———

The meaning and principles behind dopamine decor

What exactly is dopamine decor, and how does it differ from fleeting interior design fads? At its core, this style is about creating uplifting spaces that showcase your personality by surrounding yourself with treasured items that evoke happiness. Rather than catering to trends, the primary goal is to design an environment that makes you smile each day.

Unlike minimalism, which promotes sparseness and stark, neutral colors, dopamine décor fully embraces maximalism, color, sentimentality, and above all, fun. While some may call this style busy or over-the-top, that energy is precisely what makes a space distinctly you. Your home should be filled with pieces that tell your story.

The beauty of dopamine decor is that it puts personalized design over perfection. There is no checklist of rules to follow or trendy aesthetics to replicate. Instead, you simply incorporate furniture, art, colors, textures, and accessories that capture your interests, joys, and nostalgic memories. This could mean displaying your favorite books, collecting quirky ceramic creatures, or arranging family photos in colorful frames.

Leave guilt over what's fashionable behind - your space was not created to impress guests or adhere to someone else's style standards. Dopamine decor is all about letting your inner child run freely through each room, embracing the freedom to be playful, eclectic, and even wonderfully weird.

Principles of Dopamine Décor

NOW THAT WE UNDERSTAND the "why" behind dopamine decorating, let's explore the "how" by covering key guiding principles:

Focus on feelings. Above all else, every decorative choice should spark positive emotions, whether it's cheerfulness, relaxation, or nostalgia. Select pieces that make your heart sing.

Maximize color. Vibrant, saturated hues energize and uplift us, so use them abundantly through painted walls, fabrics, and accessories. Don't be afraid to go bold.

Layer in texture. Incorporate natural materials like wood and rattan along with soft textiles that beg to be touched, like velvet, corduroy, or cashmere. This adds depth and visual interest.

Display memorabilia. Curate shelves of cherished photos, collectibles, souvenirs, and keepsakes that hold sentimental value and tell your unique story.

Have fun with your space! Dopamine decorating means letting loose and not taking interior design too seriously. Don't be afraid to break design "rules" to create rooms that channel your playful spirit.

Embrace your interests. Showcase your hobbies, passions, and quirks through your design choices. Surround yourself with pieces that authentically reflect who you are.

Start small. You don't have to overhaul your entire home overnight. Test out dopamine decor with little additions like throw pillows, funky wall art, or a bright lampshade.

Mix high and low. Eclectically blending thrift store steals, hand-me-down heirlooms, personalized DIY projects, and splurge-worthy new items creates depth.

Keep organization in mind. While rich visual texture is key, don't let your space become cluttered. Use thoughtful storage to maintain a happy level of tidiness.

The most fundamental takeaway when it comes to designing a dopamine-inducing environment is this: Decorate boldly and unabashedly according to what makes your soul sing, not what's considered stylish or on-trend.

Your home should be distinctly you from the moment you walk through the front door. Surround yourself with pieces that reflect your spirit. Curate your very own feel-good space brimming with positive memories and a captivating visual feast for the senses.

It's time to take yourself off decorating autopilot and channel your inner child once more. Let color, imagination, playfulness, and nostalgia be your guides. Your home is meant to be an uplifting retreat for you alone, not a showroom. Therefore, the only style that matters is the one that brings you genuine happiness and joy every single day.

How dopamine decor promotes happiness and wellbeing

The Science Behind Dopamine Décor

WHILE THE WORD ITSELF contains "dopamine," the feel-good neurochemical, the happiness-boosting benefits of this decor style are far more than just a namesake. The strategic use of color, meaningful memorabilia, and nostalgic textures fosters positive emotions and improves overall wellbeing. Science shows that our environment directly impacts mood. Therefore, intentionally designing our homes to uplift can make a significant difference in our daily lives.

Color Psychology

THE ABUNDANT USE OF vibrant, saturated color is a hallmark of dopamine décor. But color isn't simply added for aesthetics - its selection is science-based. Studies show that different hues directly influence emotions and behaviors. Let's explore how to effectively wield the power of color:

- Yellow - This cheerful hue stimulates the release of serotonin and dopamine, bringing on a boost of happiness and confidence. Use it when you need a pick-me-up.

- Red - Associated with love, intimacy, and strength, red also raises heart rate and captures attention, making it perfect for accent walls or energizing workspace.

- Pink - Tones of pink promote relaxation and diffuse aggression and anxiety. Its gently feminine vibe is ideal for bedrooms.

- Orange - This vibrant, sunny color boosts energy and enhances mood. Use orange accessories and art for an instant dose of delight.

- Green - From mint to emerald, green evokes renewal, harmony, and freshness. Incorporate this color to cultivate peaceful spaces.

- Blue - Cool hues of blue are strongly tied to relaxation and productivity. Paint your office robin's egg blue for a soothing work environment.

- Purple - Traditionally a color of luxury and creativity, purple can awaken imagination. Use it in playrooms or home offices.

We will revisit this in the section called "Harnessing the Science of Color Psychology"

Optimism Boost

Incorporating motivational quotes, affirmation art prints, and inspiring images lifts our spirits, outlook, and self-belief. Displaying meaningful quotes, staying surrounded by positive messaging, and gazing upon uplifting photography infuses our environment with optimism and possibility.

Memory Activation

Dopamine décor leverages nostalgia by incorporating meaningful memorabilia and keepsakes that spark treasured recollections and emotions tied to fond memories. Photos of loved ones, travel souvenirs, vintage family heirlooms, and items from our childhood comfort us and conjure happy reflections.

Mental Restoration

Natural textures and cozy, soft furnishings satisfy our senses and promote deep rest and rejuvenation. Cashmere throws, velvet pillows, sheepskin rugs, live plants, and wooden accents bring natural serenity to inner-city apartments. Interacting with natural materials is mentally restoring.

Imagination Ignition

Whimsy and playfulness nurture creativity and imagination. By embracing your inner child and opting for fun, colorful, handmade, or eccentric décor, you build an environment that ignites original thought and freedom of expression. Your home should fuel your imagination, not restrain it.

Personality Showcasing

Above all, dopamine décor grants you the courage to authentically showcase your tastes and passion through every design choice. Surrounding yourself with pieces imbued with personal meaning, in colors that resonate with you, displayed in ways that channel your unique personality maximizes enjoyment of your space by creating an inspiring reflection of you.

WHILE SOCIETY MAY TRIVIALIZE the impact of interior design on wellbeing, science confirms that our environment profoundly impacts mood, outlook, and behavior. The stimulating yet soothing nature of dopamine décor caters to our psychological needs, acting as an antidepressant that you live within.

Each décor choice either contributes to your daily happiness or detracts from it. Therefore, crafting a personalized haven using colors, objects, and styles that spark nostalgia and joy is among the wisest investments you can make in your mental health and quality of life.

Here are additional ways dopamine décor benefits wellbeing:

- Increased energy and alertness from bright colors

- Reduced anxiety and depression through preferred aesthetics

- Deepened relaxation response from natural textures

- Strengthened connections between memories and emotions

- Boosted creative output in whimsical spaces

- Strengthened sense of identity from self-expression

In short, surrounding yourself with pieces imbued with personal significance, in colors and patterns that bring you delight positively impacts both psyche and emotional outlook. Dopamine décor leverages the mind-body connection between décor and wellbeing to maximize enjoyment of your living space and life overall.

The Design Elements That Define Dopamine Décor: color, texture, memorabilia

WHAT ARE THE INTEGRAL ingredients that comprise this uplifting style? Dopamine decor ultimately comes down to the strategic use of vivid color, natural texture, and nostalgic memorabilia. When used in harmony, these three design elements create living spaces that boost mood, inspire imagination, and promote authentic self-expression.

The Power of Vibrant Color

COLOR IS ARGUABLY THE quintessential visual component of dopamine décor. Rich, saturated hues applied through paint, fabric, furniture, and art inject vibrant energy into any space. The strategic use of color is what primarily sets this style apart from muted, minimalist décor.

Why is color so integral to dopamine design? Pigment has an innate ability to alter human perception, emotion, and behavior. An influx of lively hues instantly lifts one's mood. Here are specific ways to effectively incorporate color:

- Paint your walls an energetic hue like coral, mint, or yellow - Colorful walls establish an uplifting backdrop.

- Choose colorful furniture & accessories - Vibrant pillows, art, rugs, and décor enliven a room.

- Use multiple complementary colors - Pair shades like blue and orange or pink and green.

- Establish a color palette - Stick to 3-5 core hues for cohesion.

- Add pops of brightness - Use citrine and turquoise in doses for punctuation.

- Incorporate color blocked patterns - Bold geometric and graphic prints add visual dynamism.

- Experiment with different saturations - Mix muted and maxed-out shades.

- Keep the colors personal - Select hues linked to positive memories.

Remember, dopamine décor is about surround yourself with colors that make you happy, not selecting hues simply because they are deemed "in." Lean into colors that hold personal meaning or remind you of beloved places and people.

The Warmth of Natural Texture

IN ADDITION TO VIBRANT color, an abundance of natural textures is integral for creating that cozy, nostalgic atmosphere synonymous with dopamine design. Tactile layers lend a sense of depth, comfort, and inviting softness.

Natural woven fibers like jute, seagrass, cotton, and bamboo add casual texture. Cashmere, fleece, velvet, and chenille offer plush softness. Wood finishes, ceramic accents, and woven rattan contribute organic texture. Macramé wall hangings provide pure tactile intrigue.

When sourcing natural texture, prioritize pieces that seem pleasing to touch. Seek out furnishings and accents that just beg to be handled. We inherently crave touching inviting textures. Channel this draw by peppering in slubby throws, ceramic lamps, rattan poufs, and wooden bowls.

Here are more ways to effectively incorporate natural texture:

- Layer in woven blankets and shag pillows

- Select furniture with textural fabric like bouclé, terry cloth, or tweed

- Bring the outdoors in with ceramic planters and vases

- Incorporate wood elements like bowls, trays, and wall panels

- Display organic pieces like driftwood, stones, and shells

- Hang textural wall tapestries and macramé art

- Use nubby jute, seagrass, hemp rugs and baskets

- The Nostalgia of Cherished Memorabilia

The final element that defines dopamine decorating is the prominent display of nostalgic memorabilia. These sentimental items spark treasured memories and comfort us through their emotional associations.

Meaningful memorabilia you can creatively incorporate includes:

- Family photos - Frame special moments and relatives.

- Souvenirs - Display pieces that remind you of adventures.

- Collections - Exhibit any sets of objects you've gathered.

- Antiques - Upcycle your grandparents' furnishings.

- Albums - Showcase cherished records or stickers.

- Artifacts - Highlight items linked to hobbies and passions.

- Posters - Hang onto old artwork and prints.

- Childhood objects - Keep toys, books, or clothing for decoration.

The cherished memorabilia you choose to put on display should have a personal significance based on your own memories and life experiences. These special pieces imbue our homes with nostalgic emotion.

In summary, dopamine décor distinguishes itself from other styles through its unapologetic use of energizing pigment, touchable natural textures, and emotion-evoking keepsakes. When used in harmony, these three elements allow you to create personalized spaces that uplift the spirit, promote wellbeing, and celebrate what makes you undeniably you.

Chapter 2: Defining Your Decor Style

―――

Channeling Your Inner Child

As adults, we often lose touch with the freedom of self-expression and whimsy we once embodied as children. Professional, social, and cultural pressures lead us to abandon beloved aesthetics, interests, and quirks in the name of looking "mature" or "refined." But dopamine decor seeks to turn back the clock - to reconnect with the unrestrained creativity and personality of childhood that gets buried beneath the stresses of adulthood.

Your home should be a safe haven where you make zero apologies for who you are. Through your design choices, find inspiration by revisiting your younger self. Fill your space with pieces that channel the spirit of your childhood. Surround yourself with colors, patterns, textures, and objects reminiscent of joyful and nostalgic times gone by.

To connect with your childhood tastes, ask yourself:

What were my favorite colors as a kid?

• Did I obsess over rainbow hues or gravitate toward pastels? Reintroduce a beloved color palette.

What aesthetic did my childhood bedroom embody?

• Whether it was princess pink or sporty stripes, draw decor inspiration from the rooms you loved most.

Which cartoons, movies, and characters did I adore?

● Display posters, figurines, or prints showcasing beloved pop culture icons and fictional worlds from your youth.

What was my favorite toy or childhood hobby?

● Showcase meaningful items that represent your childhood passions, from Barbies to ballet shoes.

What objects bring on nostalgia?

● Surround yourself with items that prompt fond memories of your upbringing like vintage lunchboxes or boomboxes.

What inspire my imagination as a child?

● Add whimsical pieces that recapture youthful wonder like hanging chairs, hammocks, or canopy beds.

Which emotions did my childhood home fill me with?

● Choose colors and accessories that recreate feelings like joy, tranquility, excitement, or love derived from your upbringing.

While some dismiss childhood preferences as unsophisticated, dopamine décor champions unabashed self-expression. Your tastes need not remain static - they can grow and evolve with you. But first, look inward and find inspiration from the favorite colors, clothes, music, books, games, and aesthetics that set your soul alight as a child.

Many abandon treasured pieces of themselves in the quest to look more polished or refined. But surrounding yourself with pieces imbued with childlike joy and wonder keeps your spirit vibrant and your inner child alive. With your home as a safe haven, give yourself full permission to be playful, have fun, and never fully "grow up."

Here are additional ways to infuse your space with childhood whimsy:

- Display favorite childhood photos and carved initial crafts

- Frame beloved cartoon or storybook art

- Incorporate colors from crayons and markers you loved

- Hang a swing, hammock, or treehouse plywood

- Showcase favorite childhood books and movie memorabilia

- Reintroduce beloved patterns like polka dots or Toile de Jouy

- Mix in furniture from your childhood home

- Hang musical instruments you learned to play as a kid

- Exhibit trophies, medals, and awards from childhood achievements

The beauty of dopamine décor is that it encourages you to proudly showcase pieces of your inner child within your design scheme, not hide them away. Your home should spark creativity, not restrain it. Immerse yourself in aesthetics and interests central to your very identity - ones formed during your wonder years.

Honoring nostalgia and sentimental pieces

AN INTEGRAL FACET OF dopamine decor is prominently displaying nostalgic items that hold sentimental significance in your life story. The memorabilia you choose to exhibit honors heartwarming memories, pays tribute to beloved relationships, and represents treasured aspects of your identity.

Unlike mass produced décor that lacks meaning, your sentimental keepsakes have been lovingly collected over years. They prompt a flood of fond recollections and powerful emotions each time you look upon them. When artfully arranged, these cherished relics bring deeper personalization and heart to your home.

Sentimental décor can take many forms:

- Photographs - Frame nostalgic moments with family, friends, pets.

- Souvenirs - Display memorable trips and adventures.

- Trophies - Exhibit academic, athletic, career achievements.

- Collections - Showcase any sets of objects you've gathered.

- Antiques - Upcycle relatives' furniture or wedding china.

- Art - Hang onto paintings, pottery, or quilts gifted by loved ones.

- Jewelry - Display cases allow you to highlight special pieces.

- Ticket Stubs - Highlight memorable concerts, games, shows.

- Posters - Hold onto old artwork and prints that still resonate.

- Textiles - Repurpose childhood clothing or blankets.

- Plants - Keep living mementos propagated from relatives' gardens.

- Books - Showcase editions passed down through generations

- Music - Frame iconic records, album art, or concert tees.

By creatively incorporating nostalgic relics, you deepen the meaning and sentimentality of your space. Take time relishing the memories each piece evokes. Let them transport you to times, places, and relationships locked fondly in your heart. Use these sentimental accents as jumping off points for storytelling and reminiscing.

To prevent your home from feeling cluttered, thoughtfully edit your memorabilia collection and keep only pieces that hold special significance. Arrange displays in aesthetic vignettes, not haphazard piles. Lead with cherished photos and sprinkle in complementary accessories. This balances sentimentality with intent and refinement.

Your personal treasures need not be confined to private spaces out of guests' view. Tastefully worked into your décor, they become touchpoints for meaningful connections and charming story swapping. After all, surrounding ourselves with relics imbued with memory helps us celebrate our histories and very identities.

While minimalists may argue sentimental items create visual clutter, dopamine décor proves our keepsakes in fact infuse our homes with nostalgic emotion, personalization, and soul. Life is not meant to be decluttered - it is meant to be cherished. So honor each memento for the love and laughter it represents. Let your home proudly showcase the souvenirs of a life lived vibrantly.

Selecting Your Signature Color Scheme

ONE OF THE MOST PIVOTAL decisions when embracing dopamine décor is determining which vibrant color palette reflects your spirit and showcases your personality. While trendy "Color of the Year" paint hues come and go, your signature color scheme should remain true to you.

Start by revisiting meaningful colors tied to treasured memories and positive emotions. Which hues fill you with joy and come to mind when recalling beloved people, places, or times? Use these as jumping off points for selecting your core palette.

Beyond nostalgic colors, also factor in:

- Favorite Colors - Which hues have you been consistently drawn to since childhood? Stay true to longtime loves.

- Mood Enhancement - Seek out tones known to boost spirits like sunshine yellow, verdant green, and tranquil blue.

- PersonalMeaning - Choose colors representing causes or organizations important to you.

- Artwork Colors - Pull out unifying shades from cherished paintings or prints.

- Nature Inspiration - Mimic uplifting hues from stunning sunsets, landscapes, and blooms.

- Cultural Heritage - Incorporate colors celebrated within your ethnic background.

- Wardrobe Staples - Echo the palette of flattering clothing you gravitate toward.

Once you land on your core color scheme, display it abundantly throughout your home. Paint walls in your favorite tone, then layer in accent shades through textiles, accessories, and art. Upholding a coherent color story will create harmony and cohesion even when using eclectic pieces.

Here are additional tips for selecting and applying your color palette:

- Limit your palette to 3-5 core hues for cohesion.

- Showcase one dominant color, supported by complementary accent shades.

- Use color grouping and repetition to allow hues to build upon one another.

- Choose palettes with contrasting accent colors for visual dynamism.

- Incorporate patterns and textures in palette colors for depth.

- Mix sheens like matte, satin, and high-gloss in coordinated colors.

Display your color palette proudly like a badge of honor. Selecting signature shades that align with your spirit allows you to take color trends out of the equation and focus solely on curating combinations that bring you delight.

While some spaces demand conservative, neutral colors, your home offers a chance to embrace your most vibrant self through pigment. So channel your inner child once more and give yourself full creative license. After all, your living space should champion self-expression, not stifle it.

Remember, color selection deeply personal. Yours need not be universally pleasing. It simply needs to authentically resonate with your lifelong favorites, cherished memories, core values, and taste preferences. Lean into hues that rouse your spirit.

Chapter 3: Decorating with Color

———

Harnessing the Science of Color Psychology

While often overlooked, the deliberate use of color is one of the most powerful tools at your disposal for instantly shifting the overall mood and energy of a space. Extensive research confirms color directly impacts our emotions, behaviors, and physiological responses. So wielding color intentionally allows you to design feel-good environments that uplift and inspire.

Each hue possesses its own persuasive psychology and symbolism based on cultural associations and spiritual meanings accrued over centuries. While personal color preferences vary, general trends emerge:

- **Red** - This bold, passionate hue is inherently stimulating and high-energy. Red increases circulation and raises blood pressure, speeding up respiration and heart rate. It boosts excitement, appetite, and conversation, making it perfect for social spaces like dining rooms and lounges. Red provokes romance and intimacy as well, ideal for bedrooms. And it promotes productivity and focus, helpful in active workspaces.

- **Pink** - Universally associated with femininity, romance, and innocence, soft pinks have an innate sense of warmth, playfulness, and whimsy. These tender hues promote relaxation and diffuse feelings of aggression or anxiety. Light pinks create welcoming bedrooms, living rooms, and spas. Vibrant hot pinks add fun pops of color. Pink inspires nurturing vibes, ideal for children's spaces.

● **Orange** - This vibrant, cheerful hue combines the energy of red with the joy of yellow. Associated with enthusiasm and creativity, orange boosts mood, socialization, and communication. It sparks productive yet playful energy, perfect for shared workspaces. Orange adds warmth to any room. Use it to create an energetic, inspiring entryway. For kids' spaces, orange promotes learning and self-expression.

● **Yellow** - The quintessential color of sunshine, happiness, and optimism, yellow boosts serotonin and dopamine levels while activating memory and motivation. It aids concentration yet also provides relief from fatigue and anxiety. Use energetic yellow in workspaces to sharpen focus. Soft yellows create cheerful, welcoming kitchens and living rooms. Yellow inspires hope and confidence.

● **Green** - Universally associated with nature, renewal, stability, and tranquility, green possesses healing properties that reduce anxiety and promote balance. Sage greens cultivate peaceful bedrooms, while vivid greens energize exercise spaces. Green aids vision health, ideal for home offices. And it stimulates creativity, perfect for art studios. Surround yourself with green to create sanctuary.

● **Blue** - Cool, calming shades of blue lower heart rate and relax the mind, aiding concentration and inspiringreflection. Use blue in bedrooms to promote deep sleep and in offices to enhance productivity. Soft powder blues create serene, ethereal spa spaces. Navy blues lend spaces intimacy and subtle drama. Blue conjures images of soothing water.

- **Purple** - Traditionally a color of luxury, creativity, and mystery, purple provokes imagination and introspection. On the energetic side, vivid violets and fuchsia inject fun and whimsy, perfect for playrooms. Deeper eggplants and lilacs inspire contemplation and spiritual wisdom, ideal for meditation spaces. Allow purple to unlock your creativity.

Layering bright, optimistic hues establishes an uplifting backdrop while neutral walls allow accent colors to pop. When selecting your palette, consider how each hue impacts your mood and energy. Design your environment to nurture positive emotions.

Here are additional tips for effectively applying color:

- Saturate walls, textiles, and decor abundant in your favorite hues.

- Choose warmer tones like coral, peach, saffron for high-energy spaces.

- Incorporate cooler hues like sage, periwinkle, mint in relaxing spaces.

- Use darker shades to create intimate, cocooning spaces.

- Apply lighter tones in tight spaces to evoke spaciousness.

- Highlight architectural details by painting them in contrasting colors.

- Add pops of brightness with citrine, turquoise, and neon accents.

While many avoid strong color out of fear it will overwhelm, done right, it achieves the opposite - colorful rooms feel uplifting, playful, and alive. Don't shy away from boldness. Surround yourself with vibrant pigments that kindle joy.

Keep in mind that color perception depends on lighting. Use soft bulbs, illuminated paints, and natural light to make colors appear crisp yet inviting. And apply color thoughtfully in layers - don't overwhelm with competing hues in every finish and accessory. Allow each shade space to make an impact.

Above all, choose a color palette aligned with your personality and preferences, not fleeting trends. Seek out tones imbued with personal symbolism and meaning. Reestablish an emotional connection with color rooted in your childhood favorites and most treasured memories. Your home offers a chance to unapologetically embrace the hues that rouse your spirit.

Selecting Your Soul-Soothing Palette

ONE OF THE MOST PIVOTAL steps in curating feel-good spaces is defining a cohesive color palette that reflects your spirit. When choosing your signature shades, look inward to identify hues that hold deep personal meaning and elicit positive emotions.

Ask yourself:

1. Which colors spark joy and lift my mood?
2. Which tones do I associate with beloved memories and places?
3. Which hues have I been consistently drawn to since childhood?
4. Which colors align with causes or organizations I support?
5. Which shades match my complexion and flatter my skin tone?

Also extract color inspiration from:

1. Your collection of cherished artwork and prints
2. Stunning sunrises, sunsets, natural landscapes
3. Heritage flags and textiles connected to your family backgrounds
4. Your cultural traditions and celebrations

Once you've gathered inspiring colors, narrow down your signature palette to 3-5 complementary core hues. Choosing a focused color scheme creates harmony and cohesion even when decorating eclectically.

Here are ways to effectively apply your hand-picked palette:

1. Use one dominant hue throughout, supported by accent shades
2. Incorporate palette colors into wall paint, textiles, furniture, art
3. Echo colors through pattern mixing and layered textures
4. Choose a palette with contrasting accent colors for visual dynamism
5. Mix sheens like matte, satin, metallic, high-gloss in coordinated hues
6. Add warmth with wood tones and cream accents to balance bold colors

When implementing your color scheme, uphold balance and avoid overwhelming spaces with competing hues. Allow each shade room to make an impact through thoughtful grouping and repetition.

While trends come and go, your signature color palette should remain true to your spirit. Curate combinations that boost your mood and prompt fond recollections. Remember, the colors we surround ourselves with subconsciously influence our mindset and emotional state.

Here are additional tips for applying your personal palette:

1. Use light, bright hues to make small spaces feel more open
2. Incorporate darker, moodier tones in large rooms or to create intimacy
3. Paint architectural details like moldings in contrasting colors for emphasis
4. Add pops of brightness with citrine, chartreuse, fuchsia accents

5. Incorporate metallic sheens like gold, rose gold, bronze for
    warmth

The colors you choose for your home should bring you delight when
applied artfully to your walls, textiles, furnishings, and finishes.
Decorating with purposeful palettes infuses your space with positive
psychology and emotion. So embrace colors vibrantly and
unapologetically - not those dictated by trends.

Injecting Brightness with Thoughtful Accents

WHILE SATURATED WALL colors establish an uplifting backdrop, sprinkling in vivid pops of accent hues keeps spaces feeling fresh, lively, and energized. Bold and unexpected splashes of color add visual dynamism, joyfully energizing rooms anchored in lighter neutrals.

Vibrant accents add layers of interest while creating unlikely color combinations that catch the eye and spark delight. Groupings of complementary brights provide an energetic counterpoint to otherwise calm spaces.

Here are ways to artfully incorporate pops of color as accents:

- Display brightly hued artwork, textiles, ceramics to inject color

- Add bright-colored dramatic lighting like crimson or sapphire pendant lights

- Incorporate neon and fluorescent accents in framing, vases, stationery

- Paint interior doors or architectural trim in a vivid contrasting color

- Use boldly colored furnishings like emerald green velvet sofas or citron chairs

- Layer in eye-catching throw pillows, blankets, and cushions on neutral beds/sofas

- Scatter bright rug accents like hot pink sheepskins or graphic orange mats

- Choose vivid kitchen appliances and décor in shades like cobalt, vermillion, and gold

- Showcase vibrant potted botanicals like fuchsia orchids or chartreuse succulents

- Hang faceted, colorful crystal prisms near windows to cast rainbow light

---

WHEN APPLYING POPS of color:

- Focus on one accent color per room for cohesion

- Anchor brights with plenty of white and natural wood tones

- Use accents sparingly to prevent overwhelmingly spaces

- Add color in manageable doses through art, textiles, flowers

- Choose hues that complement your core color scheme

While neutrals and wood tones provide an organic, soothing foundation, vivid accents enliven rooms in subtly vibrant ways. Pops of color introduce thrilling contrast without overpowering. They provide necessary punctuation to counterbalance lighter backgrounds.

Most importantly, choose accent colors purely based on which hues elicit joy and positivity. Ignore trends and let color psychology guide your pairings. Combine tones known to lift your mood.

Squeeze every ounce of visual intrigue from your bright accents by backlighting colored glass vases and artwork or illuminating them with strategic spotlighting. This makes colors glow and appear richer. Surrounding yourself with electrifying pops boosts energy and mood while showcasing your bold spirit.

Chapter 4: Layering in Texture

———

Understanding the Power of Touch

While color and visual interest grab our attention initially, texture adds critical depth and dimension through the sense of touch. Dopamine décor leverages our human instinct to reach out and interact with pleasing textures. The addition of natural materials we crave stroking creates inviting warmth.

On a subconscious level, we are drawn to soothing, organic textures that evoke feelings of comfort, ease, and pleasure. Our minds associate tactile materials with relaxation and joy.

Consider why we flock to silk, cashmere, wood, leather, velvet, and wool:

- Soft, smooth textures relax and destress - Gentle stroking motions calm the nervous system. Caressing velvet, silk, or fleece soothes anxiety.

- Rough, nubby textures offer comfort - Coarse woven textures like bouclé fabric satisfy our craving for comforting physical touch.

- Natural textures feel innately pleasing - Materials derived from nature, like wood, cotton, and wool appeal to our senses.

- Familiar textures elicit nostalgia - Fabrics worn since childhood, like denim and linen prompt fond memories through touch.

● Novel, intriguing textures captivate us - Unusual tactile discoveries like sequins and fringe capture our curiosity.

In dopamine décor, choose pieces with pleasing physical properties you long to touch again and again. Seek out furnishings with inherent softness that entice interaction. Prioritize natural fibers, woven patterns, and cozy knits.

Here are additional ways to incorporate tantalizing textures:

● Layer plush blankets, cushions, and pillows abundantly

● Drape textural throws and sheepskins across sofas

● Incorporate nubby, dimensional upholstery fabrics like bouclé and tweed

● Display natural elements like driftwood, stones, shells

● Add softness with velvet pillows, berber rugs, chenille throws

● Incorporate wooden furniture, trays, tabletop accents

● Hang tactile wall tapestries with macramé and tassels

● Choose furniture and fabrics with handcrafted imperfections

● Gather baskets of woven raffia, seagrass, rattan

By tapping into textures you long to touch again and again, you create living spaces filled with finishing that bring you comfort and delight while appealing to your senses. Surfaces imbued with soothing tactile properties relax the body and mind.

Enveloping Your Space in Cozy Textiles

WHEN DESIGNING FOR optimal texture and comfort underfoot and atop furnishings, fabrics reign supreme. Plush rugs, cushions, pillows, throws, and upholstery invite snuggling while introducing tantalizing visual and tactile diversity.

Dopamine décor capitalizes on our affection for touchable textiles by emphasizing abundantly layered natural fibers and sumptuous knits. Time-honored materials like cotton, wool, linen, and silk add organic coziness.

Here are cozy fabrics and textiles to incorporate:

- Knit Throws - Chunky, handcrafted wool, alpaca, and cotton throws provide snug softness ideal for bed backs, sofas, and chairs. Opt for chunky knits with brushed interiors for optimal coziness.

- Woven Wool Rugs - Naturally insulating wool rugs add comforting cushioning and visual texture when underfoot. Wool's sound-absorbing properties also cut down on echos.

- Velvet Pillows - With indulgent softness begging to be touched, velvet instantly elevates sofas and beds. Look for cotton-backed velvet that won't slip around.

- Cashmere Blankets - Known for unparalleled lightness and warmth, cashmere crafts heirloom-quality blankets. Seek out Mongolian cashmere for durability.

- Mohair Throws - Made of angora goat hair, mohair possesses a fluffy, fuzzy texture perfect for cozying up in. Mohair brilliantly diffuses light, creating cozy ambiance.

- Chenille Pillows - With its signature tufted pile, chenille has an irresistibly soft, dimensional texture. Chenille resists fading, pilling, and crushing.

- Alpaca Throws - Hypoallergenic and thermal regulating, alpaca throws provide extraordinary softness. Alpaca rivals cashmere for softness at a more affordable price point.

- Llama Wool Rugs - Llama wool makes plush yet durable rugs that insulate and delight. Llama wool contains no lanolin so it won't aggravate allergies.

- Silk Pillowcases - Unquestionably luxurious and gentle against skin and hair, silk makes indulgent bedding. Mulberry silk offers the longest-lasting quality.

When sourcing fabrics, seek out natural fibres like wool, cotton, linen, and silk which feel comforting against skin. Prioritize durability and craftsmanship to build keepsakes that last generations. Shop for textiles that can be frequently laundered to maintain freshness and vibrancy.

Here are additional ways to infuse rooms with fabric texture:

1. Choose upholstery in tactile fabrics like bouclé, tweed, or corduroy
2. Layer rug textures and fabrics - flatweave under shag under sheepskin
3. Incorporate fabric wall panels, headboards, macramé wall hangings
4. Display beautifully bound books and leather goods

5. Showcase heirloom table linens, tapestries, and quilts
6. Add dimensionality with fabric draping, gathering, and ruching
7. Mix sheens like matte cotton, lustrous velvet, shiny satin

Curating a thoughtful blend of new and vintage textiles creates depth and visual interest while providing endless comfort. Limit synthetics which lack natural breathability and temperature control. The sensations of wrapping ourselves in comforting textiles satisfies our perpetual craving for coziness.

Bringing the Outdoors In with Natural Elements

IN ADDITION TO PLUSH textiles, incorporating materials straight from nature infuses spaces with cozy, organic texture and warmth. Natural accents like wood, rattan, bamboo, jute, and ceramic add delightful depth while connecting to the outdoors.

- Wood - No material is more warm, inviting, and universally beloved than wood. Salvaged wood adds rustic patina. Smooth sanded wood provides sleek contrast. Oak, walnut, teak, and mahogany all have different grains to appreciate. Use wood for shelving, furniture, flooring, and accent walls. The sound, smell, and aesthetic of wood is unparalleled.

- Rattan - With its tactile woven texture, rattan makes one-of-a-kind furnishings and accents. It has a lightweight, airy quality perfect for living spaces. Incorporate handwoven rattan headboards, cabinetry, trunks, chairs, and wall screens. The organic variations in rattan add natural beauty.

- Jute - As a fiber, jute possesses an earthy, burlap-like texture that brings cozy rusticity to any surface, from woven rugs and wall hangings to lampshade backing. Jute appeals to minimalists and maximalists alike with its neutral tones and nubby texture.

• Bamboo - Bamboo can be pressed into pliable sheets for curvy furniture or woven into airy screens and mats. Bamboo communicates tranquility and flexibility through its tactile properties. Use bamboo furnishings and decor to soften hard edges.

• Ceramic - From humble mugs to handbuilt vases, the cool, smooth, weighty texture of ceramic appeals to human senses. Ceramics bridge indoor and outdoor spaces. Work carved wooden bowls and ceramic tableware into kitchen and dining room displays.

• Concrete - While hard and industrial, concrete takes on a soothing, grounding presence when polished into tile, decorative bowls, and tabletops. Concrete adds comforting mass and permanence. Use it indoors and out for an organic yet refined look.

• Stone - Marble, travertine, granite, and other natural stones make stunning countertops, floors, walls, and decor. The visual depth, permanence, and veining found in natural stone is unparalleled. Let stone bring your spaces back to ancient roots.

When sourcing natural materials, seek out repurposed and reclaimed wood, as well as ethically harvested rattan, bamboo, and jute. Make every effort to preserve natural resources. Mixing natural textures together creates depth and dimension - pair stone tabletops with woven dining chairs, rattan carpets atop wooden flooring, ceramic planters on live edge tables. The blend of natural materials soothes the soul.

Here are more ways to infuse indoor rooms with organic accents:

- Hang woven palm leaf wall decor and bamboo window screens

- Display geode slices, agate coasters, and stone bookends

- Choose naturally dyed, undyed linen and cotton textiles

- Accent with handthrown pots and ceramic garden stools

- Illuminate spaces with room dividers, lanterns, and lamps of woven rattan or wood

- Craft wooden gallery walls to showcase art and beloved objects

- Layer cowhide rugs over jute carpeting for delightfully contrasting textures

By thoughtfully blending natural materials you source sustainably, you satisfy the inherent human craving for exposure to unrefined, tactile elements from the natural world. Their textural properties relax the mind, body, and spirit.

Chapter 5: Displaying Cherished Items

―――

Curating your memorabilia and keepsakes

More than any décor trend, the heart of dopamine design lies in proudly displaying nostalgic memorabilia imbued with sentimental significance. Curating these cherished keepsakes injects spaces with personality and soul.

Seek out mementos tied to beloved memories and relationships. Photographs, souvenirs, family heirlooms, and childhood treasures each tell part of your unique story. Artfully arrange touches from the past to inspire recollection of adventures, celebrations, and those you hold dear.

- Photographs - Frame collections of moments capturing loved ones, monumental events, and favorite faraway places. Display wedding portraits, candid family shots, or professional senior photos. Include a range of sizes, black and white alongside color. Arrange framed photos in graphic gallery walls or casual clusters. Slip some prints into books as bookmarks. Choose frames that complement your décor style.

- Childhood Art - Preserve favorite drawings, pottery, sculptures, and school art projects from your youth. Frame or display these on the refrigerator to appreciate the creativity and innocence of childhood. Your inner child will smile knowing their contributions still have a place.

● Awards & Trophies - Exhibit academic honours, sports victories, and career accomplishments via the trophies, medals, ribbons, and plaques you've accumulated. Display academic regalia like diplomas. These recognize your past efforts while motivating future achievements.

● Musical Instruments - Showcase the musical instruments you learned to play, from violins and guitars to trumpets and clarinets. Mount them or prop them in stands as artistic focal points. Let guests know you're musically inclined.

● Collections - Display any sets of objects you've gathered through the years - from stamps and coin collections to assembled pottery, antiques, or vintage clothing. Collections reflect your interests and what captures your curiosity.

● Travel Souvenirs - Demonstrate your love of adventure by exhibiting souvenirs, photos, maps, tickets, and curiosities picked up on trips near and far. Group like objects together in curiosity cabinets or shadowboxes. Share your passion for new discoveries.

● Antique Furnishings - Incorporate furniture, lighting, or decorative pieces passed down through your family. Refinish and modernize heirloom furniture by reupholstering or repainting while preserving their legacy. Let items recount your ancestry.

● Prized Books - Exhibit rare first editions or books autographed by prominent authors alongside dog-eared childhood favorites. Display them prominently on shelves or stacked on coffee tables. Let your book collection speak to your literary loves, values, and interests.

Mementos needn't be confined to private spaces – thoughtfully curated, they become delightful conversation starters and points of connection with guests. Share the significance behind each relic as you reminisce together.

When arranging your memorabilia, aim for creative displays, not cluttered piles. Thoughtfully edit pieces to only those carrying deep personal meaning. Group items into cohesive vignettes. Balance precious artifacts from the past with beloved things from the present to reflect the continuum of life.

Crafting Uplifting Photo Displays

ONE OF THE MOST POWERFUL ways to infuse spaces with sentimentality is through abundantly displaying cherished photos of loved ones, alma maters, breathtaking vistas, and monumental milestones.

Dopamine décor encourages dedicating wall space to artistically arranged collections of meaningful images that prompt happy reminiscence.

Some tips:

- Photograph Frames - Choose frames in a cohesive style like silver metal, natural wood, or black matting. Metal frames add polish while wood communicates warmth. Mix frame shapes and sizes for dynamic arrangements.

- Candid Photos - Prioritize candid shots radiating authentic joy over posed portraits for intimate glimpses into relationships. Feature generations together - old photos alongside newborns.

- Creative Arrangements - Cluster frames asymmetrically rather than grid-like. Overlap frames for dimension. Hang them salon-style clustered near one another for impact.

- Thematic Grouping - Curate mini collections around beloved themes like family holidays, beach vacations, graduations, new homes, weddings, babies, and pets.

- Black & White Photography - Incorporate both black-and-white and color photography for visual interest. Vintage black and white portraits capture timeless nostalgia.

- Enlarge Special Photos - Spotlight extra special images as large statement pieces like 16x20" enlargements. This allows their emotional impact to shine.

- Photo Books - Intersperse framed photos with displayed photobooks and albums for interactive storytelling. Leave them out to flip through.

- Everyday Moments - Don't limit yourself to monumental events - capture candid everyday moments to remember simple joys: blowing bubbles, festive meals, playground time.

- Wall Design - Use framed photos to create installation art in unique shapes like a tree, geometric collage, or heart. Arrange them to mimic wall molding.

Settings that Inspired You - Feature scenic images of places that hold special significance: honeymoon beaches, childhood homes, college campuses, sanctuaries.

Beyond cherished photographs, personalized art prints and paintings bring positivity:

- Custom Signs - Display custom street signs featuring family last names, hometowns, established dates, motivational quotes.

- House Portraits - Commission artists to recreate portraits of homes past and present, ideal above a fireplace.

- Hand-Drawn Maps - Frame artistic renderings mapping important sites and travels like weddings, hometowns, alma maters.

- Watercolor Florals - Frame vivid painting of favorite flowers and botanicals. Vibrant blossoms represent growth.

- Uplifting Quotes - Add artwork and canvases spotlighting motivational quotes that lift your outlook and beliefs.

- Nostalgic Prints - Seek old-fashioned prints featuring beloved icons like vintage cars and historic landmarks.

- Song Lyrics - Frame meaningful stanzas from songs holding personal significance as artistic reminders.

By surrounding yourself with imagery tied to beloved times, places, accomplishments, and people, you infuse your space with nostalgic positivity. Display photos artfully to spotlight what matters most. Choose frames and arrangements amplifying the mood you desire - playful, peaceful, exuberant, cozy.

Most importantly, refresh your displays seasonally. Rotate in new moments captured across the years. Allow collections to evolve as life's adventures continue unfolding. Let your walls visually recount stories while inspiring the days yet to come.

Proudly Displaying Cherished Collections

DOPAMINE DÉCOR ENCOURAGES proudly exhibiting personally curated collections that reflect your passions, interests, values and memories.

Displayed thoughtfully, assembled objects tell rich stories while revealing what captivates you.

When showcasing collections:

- Edit mindfully - Evaluate entire collections but selectively display most meaningful pieces. Avoid clutter.

- Organize logically - Group collection items together by type, date, color, size or theme.

- Elevate favorites - Spotlight particularly special pieces on their own pedestals or in framed cases.

- Label discreetly - Use small tags or plaques to identify pieces and their origin stories.

- Rotate seasonal - Refresh collection displays periodically to appreciate forgotten pieces.

- Illuminate dramatically - Use lighting to spotlight collectibles and amplify their details.

- Enhance interactivity - Allow visitors to gently handle collectibles to forge connections.

Types of collections you can proudly display:

- Memorabilia - Showcase ticket stubs, programs, pins, and other souvenirs from cherished events and travels.

- Coins & Stamps - Exhibit visually arresting coin and stamp collections in specialty albums and under glass frames.

- Figurines - Display collections of cherished figurines and statuettes, from Hummels to Precious Moments.

- Music Loves - Frame concert posters, vintage records, and signed albums from favorite bands.

- Sports Treasures - Display signed balls, jerseys, and equipment from favorite sports teams and athletes.

- Nature Finds - Create artistic arrangements of shells, stones, sand dollars, feathers, and driftwood discovered on adventures.

- Movie Memorabilia - Showcase ticket stubs, posters, autographed scripts and merch from beloved films.

- Historical Relics - Preserve interesting documents like newspapers announcing major events and old maps.

- Toys & Games - Proudly display favorite childhood games, trading cards, and iconic toys like LEGO sets.

- Books - Organize book collections by genre, subject, or color. Feature autographed editions and classics.

By proudly showcasing objects reflecting your interests, skills, values and origins, you surround yourself with daily inspiration while providing guests glimpses into your heart and spirit.

Collections represent accomplishments amassed gradually through determination. They communicate wisdom acquired, destinations reached, mementos gathered. Each piece tells a story. Each set formed reveals concentrated effort.

To prevent collections from appearing cluttered:

1. Curate designated display spaces like shadowboxes, cabinets, shelves
2. Limit collections to specific areas rather than scattering pieces throughout
3. Choose cohesive display vessels like baskets, frames, vessels in one color family
4. Arrange collections in orderly groupings - symmetrical or rainbow-ordered
5. Provide sufficient negative space around and between displayed objects
6. Adjust lighting to amplify collection details

With thoughtful presentation, collections become artistic installations expressing your essence. The act of assembling treasured sets helps satisfy our intrinsic need for gathering, organizing, and revisiting objects that sparked joy.

Surprisingly, displaying collections prominently can strengthen focus and productivity. Visually reviewing cherished collections reminds you of accomplishments attained through determination. This motivates ongoing pursuit of purpose.

Let your collections speak on your behalf, telling the story of who you are, where you've been and what you love most. Their presentation style reflects your personality while conversing on your behalf when you have guests.

Chapter 6: Pulling It All Together

Tying spaces together with color palettes

When embracing an eclectic blend of cherished memorabilia, global antiques, and vivid pops of color, upholding harmony can be challenging. The final step in curating a joyful home is pulling disparate spaces together visually using cohesive color palettes.

Implementing a consistent color scheme provides the common thread stitching rooms into a unified story even when décor varies wildly.

Here are tips for creating flow:

- Choose 3-5 core hues - Limit your signature palette to a few complementary colors.

- Apply colors repeatedly - Use accent shades consistently in all spaces.

- Establish a neutral foundation - Tie rooms together with shared neutral walls/floors.

- Echo colors in textiles - Use pillows, rugs, drapes in palette colors.

- Incorporate corresponding patterns - Unify rooms with matching geometric or floral prints.

- Maximize matching metals & woods - Repeat brass, blackened steel, walnut throughout.

• Coordinate accessories consistently - Use matching vases, trays, candlesholders.

With a harmonious color story guiding décor choices, you grant yourself the freedom to incorporate meaningful memorabilia, vivid artwork, and treasured antiques while still maintaining a feeling of zen and harmony.

Ways to expertly apply a cohesive color palette:

• Paint architectural details - Use accent colors on moldings, ceilings, interior doors.

• Tie together adjacent rooms - Paint adjoining walls shared hues or hang coordinated art.

• Establish bright focal points - Paint indoor entry doors bold accent colors.

• Create colorblocking - Use different brights in blocks on gallery walls.

• Add vibrant window dressings - Hang patterned drapes in signature shades.

• Welcome guests with color - Paint front doors energizing hues.

• Define separate zones - Use different palette colors in each family member's lounge area.

While some spaces like bedrooms cater to individual preferences, upholding one refined palette between public living areas and entryways creates a welcoming flow.

With abundant vibrant hues, thoughtful repetition is key. Echo colors in slipcovered dining chairs, accent pillows, foyer rugs, and art to prevent disjointed rainbow rooms. Aim for purposeful splashes of color not chaotic explosions.

Of course, as seasons and moods change, feel free to rotate accent pieces in new corresponding colors if original hues no longer spark joy. Just maintain a few key signature shades as the common thread.

If particular palette colors hold deep nostalgic meaning, describe their significance to guests. For example, sunshine yellow kitchen walls represent the color of your grandmother's home. This personal symbolism makes the color especially uplifting.

While some spaces work best in conservative, neutral palettes, don't fear vibrant color. Thoughtfully united colors invigorate the spirit. Just take care to apply accent shades judiciously in highlighting doses so they dazzle rather than overwhelm.

Soon your signature palette will provide that crucial feeling of home. Walking in the front door, you'll breathe a contented sigh as surrounding signature colors wash over you like a warm embrace.

Achieving balance between nostalgia and minimalism

FOR SOME, ROOMS BRIMMING with sentimental keepsakes may feel cluttered or overwhelming. When embracing nostalgic dopamine decor, aim to strike a harmonious balance with edited minimalism.

Display your most treasured memorabilia, but with plenty of breather space. Follow these tips:

- Limit frame clusters to special accent walls. Keep remaining walls streamlined.

- Showcase collections and photos within framed shadowboxes for contained displays.

- Arrange sentimental displays in neat groupings rather than scattering pieces randomly.

- Hang a few meaningful pieces of art rather than overloading walls.

- Keep surfaces like mantels and tabletops minimally decorated, changing pieces seasonally.

- Store the bulk of your memorabilia edited out of rotation. Cycle special items in and out.

- Choose sleek frames and display vessels to contrast with personal relics.

- Incorporate nostalgic elements thoughtfully into neutral, modern spaces instead of overly-ornate retro rooms.

- Uphold organization - Use matching boxes, albums, and containers to neatly store cherished items not on display.

While dopamine décor celebrates sentimentality, restraint is needed to prevent spaces from feeling dark, cluttered, or suffocating. The goal is uplifting reminiscence, not hoarding.

When curating memorabilia vignettes:

1. Edit pieces to only your most emotionally uplifting relics. Cherish through minimalism.
2. Arrange displays with plenty of negative space around and between pieces.
3. Limit grouping to intentional tableaus rather than overwhelming entire rooms.
4. Choose sleek vessels like frames and shadowboxes to corral pieces.
5. Showcase memorabilia against neutral backdrops for balance.
6. Rotate extras in and out of storage to refresh displays seasonally.

The combination of pared-back neutral foundations with pops of vibrant color, playful textures, and meaningful memorabilia strikes an ideal balance. You control the nostalgia-to-minimalism ratio depending on your comfort level.

While your home should indeed surround you with cherished keepsakes, the space still requires room to breathe, move and evolve. Cluttered rooms with dark colors can drag mood down. Bright, edited spaces allow your collections to shine.

For most uplifting results, reminisce through a refined lens. Limit sentimental styles like chintz florals, ornate frames, frilly accents. Instead, honor special relics by choosing clean-lined vessels like floating ledge shelves, geometric shadowboxes, and sleek metal frames. This keeps the focus on the irreplaceable personal pieces themselves.

Your home should spotlight the people, places, interests, and values making you who you are - but with care not to overwhelm. Thoughtfully curate and display your most precious memorabilia against a flexible backdrop embracing both beloved collections and wide open spaces.

Preserving Order Within Fullness

WHILE RICHLY LAYERED dopamine decor revels in abundance, restraint is required to prevent our spaces from becoming cluttered and overwhelming havens of hoarding.

Embrace edited maximalism by upholding mindful organization strategies allowing each treasured piece room to shine.

Here are ways to inject spaciousness while making the most of your décor:

- Limit furniture to only essential, multipurpose pieces. Choose designs accommodating integrated storage.

- Stick to one or two statement pieces per room. Allow substantial empty space around furnishings.

- Arrange furniture asymmetrically rather than pushed against walls. Float pieces to keep the center open.

- Build ample shelving and cabinets to stow items when not in use. Conceal clutter.

- Use neutral wall colors and flooring as palate cleansers between vibrant décor.

- Showcase collections and memorabilia in neatly organized displays. Contain pieces within frames and shadowboxes.

- For open floor plans, zone spaces through color, lighting and rugs rather than permanent dividers. Keep sightlines open.

- Make the most of vertical space through tall shelving and wall displays. Get visual weight off floors.

- Incorporate mirrors and reflective accents to create the illusion of more space.

- Take a minimalist approach to surfaces like console tables, mantels and nightstands. Keep them highly edited.

- Use multipurpose furniture like storage ottomans and coffee tables to add function. Nest occasional tables.

While dopamine decor grants you permission to fully embrace your passions through surrounding yourself with meaningful memorabilia, collections, vivid colors, and playful prints, upholding organization prevents spaces from becoming overwhelming. Make room to breathe.

Aim to create a sense of curation rather than accumulation. Thoughtfully edited abundance and artful disorder that appears intentional is key.

When arranging your home:

1. Group like items together in neat collection. Contain them within frames, boxes, or displays.
2. Choose storage furnishings that hide items when not in use like trunks, cabinets, and shelving units with doors.
3. For collections, rotate pieces in and out seasonally so they don't accumulate chaotically over time.
4. Prevent flat surfaces from becoming cluttered catchalls. Keep

only a few accents in each area.

5. Use calm wall colors as neutral backdrops so vivid pieces pop rather than compete.

6. Incorporate large statement pieces sparingly. Allow substantial negative space around and between furnishings.

7. The beauty of dopamine décor is fully surrounding yourself with things that make your spirit soar. But focus on quality over quantity. Cultivate a curated gallery of your most uplifting items displayed artfully. A touch of restraint preserves the magic.

Conclusion: Final Thoughts on Surrounding Yourself with Joy

If you've made it to this final chapter, you now possess everything you need to infuse your home with happiness by embracing the spirit of dopamine decor. You understand how surrounding yourself with purposeful colors, nostalgic keepsakes, cozy textures, and meaningful memorabilia can uplift your spirit and promote wellbeing.

While trends will come and go, the tips within this book focus on timeless principles of crafting spaces that reflect the unique light within you. Your home provides a sanctuary where you are free to unapologetically celebrate your passions, interests, loves and quirks through symbolic décor.

Remember, dopamine decorating grants you full permission to:

- Paint your walls in colors that lift your mood, evoke beloved memories, and bring you energy. Choose hues that make your soul sing.

- Incorporate playful patterns and prints, from polka dots to preppy plaids, that prompt smiles. Pattern boosts mood.

- Display cherished photos, souvenirs, childhood mementos, and heirlooms proudly. Surround yourself with nostalgia.

- Showcase any collections and treasures that speak to your interests proudly. Let your displayed objects tell your story.

- mix timeless natural textures like wood, rattan, ceramic, and cozy textiles abundantly to create warmth.

- Blend styles fearlessly - modern and antique, sleek and ornate, maximalist and minimalist. The blend reflects you.

- Ignore trends and decorating "rules." Let colors, furnishings, and decor that make you happiest guide all choices.

While some home aesthetics aim for universal appeal, dopamine décor champions self-expression and personal resonance above all else. Surround yourself with pieces imbued with positive memories, radiating welcoming energy, and reflecting your spirit.

Of course, with great décor freedom comes great responsibility. Artful arrangement and thoughtful restraint keep whimsical spaces from becoming overwhelming. We touched on organization strategies like:

1. Upholding cohesive color palettes to tie eclectic spaces together
2. Striking a balance between minimalism and nostalgic keepsakes
3. Containing treasured collections within frames and displays
4. Allowing breathing room around and between furnishings
5. Layering in sentimental memorabilia judiciously against neutral backdrops

The goal is crafting a personalized haven that feels curated, not cluttered. Edit abundance with care.

As you move forward, don't let decorating become a point of stress or perfectionism. Simply build your home gradually, adding special finds over time that make your day brighter. Start small with a cheerful accent wall or collection of nostalgic framed photos.

Above all, listen to your inherent sense of wonder and play. Allow your living space to showcase your inner child while representing the adult you've become. Let go of outside opinions. Decorate unapologetically according to what brings you joy, serenity, inspiration, or comfort.

Remember, a home filled with pieces imbued with personal significance, favorite colors, and meaningful memorabilia is a happy home. Your dwellings are meant to replenish you, not impress others.

Wishing you a future brimming with playful decorating adventures! May the tips within this book guide you to create havens as unique and vibrant as your spirit. Moving forward, listen to your intuition and lean into displays that resonate most with your inner light.

You now hold the blueprint for surrounding yourself with uplifting décor allowing you to live happily, authentically, and unapologetically as your best self each day. Embrace the freedom to decorate distinctly.

Whenever you need inspiration, return to the permission granted within these pages: to craft joyful spaces reflecting the color, whimsy, comfort, and meaning that sings to your soul. Create a sanctuary where you feel free to be yourself.

You've got this! Wishing you profound peace and daily happiness in the haven you cultivate.

Bonus 1 : Dopamine Nation Analysis And Key Learning

The neuroscience behind pleasure and addiction

In her pivotal book "Dopamine Nation," psychiatrist Dr. Anna Lembke illuminates the neuroscience underlying our brain's complex pleasure and reward circuitry. She explains how the neurotransmitter dopamine governs how we experience gratification.

When we bite into a fudgy ganache-filled bonbon, slide into a warm bath, or get a promotion at work, our dopamine levels spike, signaling reward. Our brains catalogue these feel-good activities, reinforcing behaviors that release more happy chemicals.

But just like building up any tolerance, we soon need more sugar, soaks, and success to get the same rush. Our receptors desensitize to once-pleasurable things. Normal joys fade into humdrum habit, driving us to seek bigger thrills to rouse our dampened dopamine response.

In today's era of endless on-demand stimulation, we're constantly bombarded with hyper-rewarding inputs deliberately designed to hijack our feel-good reward circuitry. Junk food, drugs, social media, porn, shopping splurges - all provide supra-normal stimuli engineered to cause surging dopamine release. But what goes up must come down.

Each fleeting high gives way to a rebound crash as our neurotransmitters recalibrate. Yet we soon crave another hit to quell the unease. And so the vicious cycle continues.

This phenomenon of hedonic adaptation explains why we end up numbed to pleasures that once delighted us. Our insatiable brains keep demanding ever-greater thrills merely to capture prior levels of satisfaction. But this dopamine-depleting arms race leaves us depleted, depressed, and continually wanting more.

According to Lembke, simply eliminating addictive substances or behaviors often proves ineffectual if underlying issues remain unresolved.

Without addressing deep-seated trauma, mental health struggles, or genetic and environmental factors, the addiction whack-a-mole continues. Recovery requires holistic treatment of the whole person, inside and out.

To counteract this endless drive for the next short-lived high, Lembke advocates recalibrating our reward system by swapping quick fixes for more mindful joys. Meditation, exercise, immersion in nature, and meaningful social connections may stimulate less intense dopamine spikes, but their benefits compound and endure. When we reset our hedonic set point and savor simpler pleasures, cravings for constant empty novelty subside. We discover fulfillment in stillness.

So in decorating and in life, seek balance. Limit aimless dopamine-chasing and make space for reflection. Cherish nostalgia's sweetness but don't become stuck chasing the past. Combine beloved collections with optimistic future visions. Design comfortable sanctuaries and also wide-open spaces that invite fresh possibility. Look beyond the quick hit to find beauty in subtle, lasting joys that nourish your spirit every day.

8 Key Takeaways To Be Applied Daily:

1. **Understand the Role of Dopamine:** Dopamine is a neurotransmitter responsible for the feeling of pleasure and reward. Overexposure to stimuli that cause dopamine surges can lead to decreased sensitivity and increased craving for more intense experiences.

1. **Recognize the Influence of Modern Society:** We live in a society saturated with highly pleasurable and addictive stimuli like fast food, drugs, social media, and pornography. These stimuli can hijack our reward system and create a cycle of overindulgence and addiction.

1. **Adopt a Holistic Approach to Addiction:** Addiction is a complex issue influenced by various factors, including genetics, childhood experiences, and social environment. Addressing addiction requires a comprehensive approach that considers the individual's whole life.

1. **Practice Hedonic Recalibration:** Rebalance your brain's reward system by reducing exposure to highly pleasurable and addictive stimuli. Replace these with activities that provide more sustainable and meaningful sources of pleasure, such as exercise, meditation, and social connections.

1. **Mindfulness and Self-Reflection:** Practice mindfulness and self-reflection to develop a healthier relationship with pleasure and reward. Recognize your triggers and vulnerabilities and develop strategies to manage them effectively.

1. **Prioritize Relationships:** Cultivate meaningful social connections, as they play a crucial role in maintaining mental health and well-being. Strong relationships can provide a source of support, fulfillment, and pleasure that is more sustainable and healthy than artificial stimuli.

1. **Embrace a Balanced Lifestyle:** Adopt a balanced and sustainable approach to pleasure and reward. This includes re-evaluating the role of technology and social media in your life, promoting healthier lifestyles, and creating an environment that prioritizes mental health and well-being.

1. **Gratitude and Acceptance:** Practice gratitude for the small and simple pleasures in life. Accept that pain and discomfort are natural parts of life and that seeking constant pleasure and reward can lead to imbalance and addiction.

Bonus 2: Dopamine Detox

Understanding Dopamine

Dopamine is one of our brain's crucial neurotransmitters, playing a central role in motivation, focus, and feelings of pleasure and reward. When dopamine levels spike, we experience that delightful rush signaling our brain to repeat enjoyable activities. From savoring a gooey dessert to getting a promotion at work, dopamine provides that little burst of satisfaction when we do something rewarding.

But problems arise when our reward circuitry gets overstimulated. In today's world of endless on-demand indulgences like junk food, drugs, social media, porn, and online shopping, our brains are constantly bombarded with dopamine-releasing stimuli. With overexposure, our dopamine receptors start to downregulate, becoming less responsive to everyday pleasures.

We begin needing bigger and better hits just to register the same level of enjoyment. A single scoop of ice cream stops satisfying us, so we devour the whole pint tub to recapture that initial dopamine delight. Social media likes that once thrilled us start feeling meaningless without an endless stream of notifications. This phenomenon is called hedonic adaptation - our baseline happiness keeps ratcheting up, demanding ever stronger inputs to reach the same rewarding feeling.

This insatiable drive for novelty and intensity leaves us stuck on a dopamine-depleting hamster wheel, seeking our next fix but finding less fulfillment. Our overstimulated receptors numb us to the small wonders already surrounding us. The rose loses its scent.

To break this vicious cycle of chasing bigger highs, we need to reset our dopamine levels and resensitize our reward circuitry. Enter: the dopamine detox.

What is Dopamine Detox

THE CONCEPT OF A "DOPAMINE detox" has gained popularity as a way to temporarily cut back on dopamine-triggering stimuli and allow your brain's receptors to recalibrate. The premise is straightforward: by taking a break from intensely pleasurable indulgences, you can renew sensitivity to more subtle joys and break free of dependency on novelty and excess.

A dopamine detox essentially involves:

1. Limiting exposure to hyper-stimulating activities and inputs
2. Choosing simpler, more mindful pleasures instead
3. Giving your dopamine receptors a chance to reset and recover

By avoiding addictive behaviors and stimuli for a period of time - say a weekend or a week - proponents believe you can hit the reset button on your brain's reward system. This may help restore a baseline happiness set point so you regain appreciation for ordinary pleasures often drowned out by overstimulation.

What does refraining from intense dopamine hits look like in practice? Here are some activities to temporarily limit during a detox:

1. Binging hyper-palatable foods like sugar, salt and junk food
2. Marathon gaming, TV, YouTube or porn sessions
3. Doomscrolling social media feeds for hours
4. Online shopping binges for instant gratification
5. Compulsively checking texts, emails, alerts for fresh notifications

Instead, you would spend time on more mindful activities like:

- Going for walks outdoors without your phone

- Reading books or listening to podcasts

- Creative hobbies like drawing, playing music

- Socializing with friends and family without distractions

- Cooking and eating nutritious whole foods

- Exercising, stretching and meditating

The goal isn't to deprive yourself or create suffering. It's to trade quick dopamine rushes for slower-burning satisfactions. By hitting pause on intense stimulation, we rediscover steadier sources of meaning and joy already within us. We rekindle our natural curiosity and capacity for presence.

Dopamine Detox Tips

IF YOU WANT TO EXPERIMENT with a dopamine detox, here are some tips for an effective and sustainable reset:

• Set a timeframe - Figure out a manageable period for your detox, like a weekend or a few days free of intense commitments. Extend as feels right.

• Start slow - Ease into limiting stimuli vs suddenly going cold turkey, which tends to backfire. Taper usage at a steady pace.

• Keep it tech-free - Turn off notifications and remove apps from your homescreen. Disable auto-plays and recommendations to avoid rabbit holes.

• Plan ahead - Have alternative activities lined up like hikes, books, arts and crafts projects to fill your time.

• Get support - Enlist friends and family to join your detox or at least understand your need for space.

• Avoid triggers - Stay away from tempting locations like malls or heavily trafficked city centers.

• Reward yourself - Plan a special outing, meal or treats after your detox time as something to look forward to.

• Focus on additions, not just subtractions - Try new hobbies, routines and healthy habits rather than solely focusing on restricting pleasure.

• Pay attention - Note how your energy, concentration and mood shift, for better or worse.

• Be compassionate - Don't beat yourself up for lapses. Progress happens gradually. Reset when needed.

• Customize your approach - Your detox plan will be unique. Adapt as you discover what works best for you long-term.

While the research on dopamine fasting's effects is limited, many self-report feeling more present, focused and grateful after taking a break from overstimulation. The key is finding balance - not demonizing all pleasures, but being mindful of how certain activities truly serve you.

Rather than a quick fix, consider a dopamine detox a helpful reset when you've fallen into unhealthy dependency on stimulation. Use the clarity it provides to build more sustainable habits and routines that nourish you.

The goal of any cleanse should be lasting awareness, not perfection. By periodically challenging your relationship with reward and pleasure, you gain wisdom around your needs and patterns. Resensitize yourself to life's subtle splendors.

Bonus 3 : Dopamine Agonists

D opamine is an essential neurotransmitter that activates our brain's pleasure and reward circuitry. Agonists are compounds that mimic and boost the effects of neurotransmitters. So dopamine agonists are drugs that bind to dopamine receptors and stimulate them, ramping up dopamine activity in the brain.

By increasing dopamine signaling at the receptor level, these compounds can offer therapeutic benefits related to mood, movement, and neurological conditions. Dopamine agonists provide targeted relief by acting as surrogate keys fitting into the brain's specialized dopamine locks.

When our natural dopamine production declines, sending neural signals awry, dopamine agonists can step in to pick up the slack. Like a boost of revitalizing caffeine for our lagging dopamine systems, these drugs activate feel-good dopaminergic pathways when our own neurotransmitters fall short.

From easing Parkinson's symptoms to stabilizing prolactin levels, the carefully calibrated effects of prescription dopamine agonists allow them to play a powerful role in regulating brain function. Understanding these substances provides insight into how we can harness dopamine's gifts purposefully.

By exploring how synthetic and natural compounds act at receptor sites to augment dopamine neurotransmission, we illuminate the nuanced dynamics between neurotransmitters, receptors, and essential brain processes governing our health and wellbeing. Let's dive deeper!

Exploring the Major Categories of Dopamine Agonists

WHEN OUR BRAINS' NATURAL dopamine production falls out of harmonious balance, there are several classes of receptor-binding medications we can use to pick up the slack. Let's explore the major categories of dopamine agonists in depth:

Dopamine Precursors

SOME OF THE MOST WIDELY used dopamine-boosting compounds are amino acid precursors that our bodies readily convert into dopamine itself.

L-DOPA, also known as levodopa, is an especially popular precursor because it easily crosses the blood-brain barrier before getting synthesized into dopamine. Our brains recognize L-DOPA as the raw ingredient for cooking up more of our deficient feel-good neurotransmitter.

Think of taking L-DOPA as analogous to tossing tyrosine, the amino acid building block for dopamine, right into our neurochemical kitchen. Our enzymatic chefs get to work whipping up fresh dopamine molecules.

By increasing levels of dopamine's direct precursor, we can renew depleted reserves of the essential signaling molecule. L-DOPA preparations like Sinemet are therefore standard treatments for dopamine deficiency disorders like Parkinson's disease.

Non-Ergoline Dopamine Receptor Agonists

WHILE PRECURSORS AIM to increase overall dopamine levels, other agonists directly stimulate dopamine receptors instead. These synthetic compounds activate the receptors without metabolizing into dopamine itself.

Non-ergoline agonists like pramipexole, ropinirole, and rotigotine are chemically unrelated to ergot alkaloids. This differentiated structure allows more targeted receptor binding with fewer side effects compared to ergoline agonists.

Pramipexole (Mirapex) preferentially stimulates the D3 subtype of dopamine receptor and is used for treating Parkinson's and restless leg syndrome. Ropinirole (Requip) has affinity for both D2 and D3 receptors and therefore also aids multiple conditions.

The rotigotine transdermal patch (Neupro) enables continuous dopamine receptor activation by steadily delivering the drug through the skin. This round-the-clock stimulation can smooth out inconsistent symptom relief.

Ergoline-Derived Dopamine Agonists

ERGOLINES LIKE BROMOCRIPTINE, cabergoline, and pergolide come from ergot alkaloids, compounds derived from the ergot fungus. While effective receptor binders, they are more likely to cause side effects due to their interaction with additional receptors for other neurotransmitters like serotonin.

Bromocriptine (Parlodel) was the first ergoline agonist approved and is used for treating hormone imbalances like hyperprolactinemia as well as Parkinson's. Cabergoline (Dostinex) has a very long half-life, requiring less frequent dosing.

Lisuride and pergolide were initially popular agonists but became less prescribed due to risk of cardiac valve problems. However, new extended-release preparations aim to provide symptom relief with reduced side effects.

As research on these complex compounds continues, we are discovering safer ways to fine-tune dopamine system functioning. Tailoring dopaminergic therapy to each patient's needs can restore harmony in runaway or deficient neurotransmitter activity.

The Multifaceted Medical Applications of Dopamine Agonists

DOPAMINE AGONISTS HAVE emerged as frontline treatments for an array of conditions involving dysfunctional dopamine signaling and hormone regulation. Let's dig deeper into some of their major FDA-approved and off-label uses:

Treating Parkinson's Disease

ONE OF THE MOST WELL-established uses of dopamine agonists is managing motor symptoms of Parkinson's disease like tremor, rigidity, bradykinesia, and postural instability. Because Parkinson's involves the loss of dopamine-producing neurons, directly stimulating receptors can compensate.

Dopamine precursors like levodopa and carbidopa are standards of care, along with dopamine receptor agonists like pramipexole, ropinirole, rotigotine, apomorphine, and bromocriptine. Used together, these drugs provide continuous activation of dopaminergic pathways disrupted in Parkinson's. Extended release and controlled release preparations help maintain stable symptom control.

Managing Restless Legs Syndrome

DOPAMINE AGONISTS OFFER relief for patients with moderate to severe restless legs syndrome (RLS). Pramipexole and ropinirole are FDA-approved as RLS treatments due to their efficacy for reducing unpleasant sensations and the urge to move the legs. These drugs enhance dopamine signaling in areas implicated in RLS like the substantia nigra.

Prolactinomas and Pituitary Tumors

Dopamine receptor activation in the pituitary gland decreases prolactin secretion from lactotroph cells. Therefore, ergoline agonists like bromocriptine and cabergoline are highly effective treatments for hyperprolactinemia caused by prolactinomas and other prolactin-secreting pituitary tumors.

These dopamine agonists can reduce tumor size, inhibit prolactin production, and eliminate symptoms like amenorrhea, galactorrhea, reduced bone density, and hypogonadism. Cabergoline is especially useful due to its long half-life enabling less frequent dosing.

Fibromyalgia, Depression, Addiction, and More

WHILE NOT YET FDA-APPROVED, early research indicates dopamine agonists like pramipexole may also benefit disorders like fibromyalgia, treatment-resistant depression, and substance addictions. Their dopamine-stimulating effects show therapeutic potential for certain neuropsychiatric conditions.

However, more research is needed to fully elucidate the mechanisms. Risks like increased gambling behaviors also require consideration. But as our understanding of dopamine's nuanced roles deepens, we are discovering promising new applications for precision-targeted dopamine agonists.

How Dopamine Agonists Exert Their Effects in the Brain

DOPAMINE AGONISTS PROVIDE therapeutic benefit by directly binding to and activating dopamine receptor subtypes, particularly D2 and D3 receptors. Let's unpack their mechanisms of action:

Binding Dopamine Receptors

THE BASIC PREMISE UNDERLYING dopamine agonists' effects is that they bind to specific dopamine receptor sites on neurons as an agonist would.

Some like bromocriptine have high affinity for D2 receptors while others like pramipexole preferentially bind D3. When they attach, this stimulates the receptor in the same way that dopamine would, initiating events inside the cell.

Mimicking Dopamine's Actions

BY DOCKING DIRECTLY onto dopamine receptors, agonists mimic the effects of dopamine binding at that site. Their chemical structure allows them to act as dopaminergic signaling molecules.

Essentially, dopamine agonists fool the receptors into thinking they are dopamine. This prompts the same downstream cellular changes, like second messenger system activation, that dopamine triggers.

Boosting Dopamine Signaling

WHEN OUR BRAINS' DOPAMINE production falters, taking a dopamine agonist can compensate by amplifying signaling at the receptor level.

It's like turning up the volume on a stereo when the power starts running low - the music might be quieter, but boosting the output amplifies the signal. Similarly, agonists enhance dopamine's effects when deficits occur.

This mechanism effectively counteracts conditions involving low dopamine states like Parkinson's disease and restless leg syndrome. By bypassing the need for dopamine release and directly stimulating receptors, agonists boost neurotransmission.

However, in disorders like schizophrenia that involve dopamine excess, antagonists that block receptors may be preferred. The key is rectifying imbalanced signaling.

In essence, dopamine agonists act as molecular mimics of our main "feel good" neurotransmitter. By binding and activating receptors, they can amplify, inhibit, modulate, and fine-tune dopaminergic signaling in nuanced ways. This chemical key-in-lock mechanism powers their therapeutic effects.

Understanding this receptor pharmacology sheds light on how we can precisely adjust neurotransmitter messaging using specially-crafted synthetic and natural compounds. Wielding these tools, we can potentially unlock dopamine's gifts with enhanced precision

The Exciting Frontiers of Dopamine Agonist Research and Drug Development

AS OUR KNOWLEDGE OF dopamine signaling expands, researchers are continually developing promising new dopamine agonists and exploring their potential applications. What does the future of these drugs look like?

Novel Dopamine Agonists

SEVERAL NEXT-GENERATION dopamine receptor activators are in the pipeline, including:

- ABT-724 - This highly selective D2 agonist is in Phase 1 trials for treating Parkinson's and restless legs. It aims to provide symptom relief with reduced side effects.

- AZD-1962 - An orally available D2/D3 agonist now in Phase 1b trials for treating Parkinson's symptoms. As a controlled release agent, it may provide smoother, sustained effects.

- STD-101 - A potential first-in-class D1 dopamine receptor selective compound now in preclinical development. Stimulating D1 may enhance neuroplasticity and cognitive function.

- D-512 - A plant-based D2 agonist derived from the alkaloid Annona muricata is in preclinical research for Parkinson's treatment with a lower side effect profile.

These novel agents aim to build upon the success of marketed dopamine agonists by optimizing receptor targeting, drug delivery, and side effect reduction. Developing selective compounds that activate specific dopamine receptor subtypes holds promise for customized treatment.

Treating Addiction

EARLY RESEARCH INDICATES dopamine agonists like pramipexole and bromocriptine may help treat substance addictions by normalizing dysregulated dopamine circuits involved in reward pathways and cravings. Controlled trials are examining their effectiveness and safety profiles.

The dopamine stabilizing effects of these drugs coupled with psychosocial interventions could potentially rebalance addiction-altered neurochemistry. However, more data is needed regarding risks like medication abuse.

Managing ADHD

STIMULATING DOPAMINE activity in the underactive mesocorticolimbic circuits implicated in ADHD is an emerging concept. Some researchers hypothesize gentle dopamine agonists may enhance motivation and impulse control without amphetamine-like overstimulation.

While still highly speculative, selective D2 or D4 agonists could theoretically improve ADHD symptoms like inattention, hyperactivity, and executive dysfunction more smoothly than stimulants. But clinical evidence is still sparse.

The applications reviewed here represent only a sample of the avenues currently being explored with dopamine agonists. As research continues unpacking dopamine's diverse roles in mental health, motor function, hormone regulation, and more, so too will the possibilities for precision drug targeting.

It is an exciting time to be at the frontiers of dopamine agonist development as our understanding of receptor pharmacology matures. The future continues to hold great promise for harnessing and fine-tuning dopamine's gifts therapeutically via designed drug-receptor interactions. With biochemistry leading the way, we edge closer to balanced brain communication.

Calling All Décor queens: We Need Your Help!

Now that you've joined me on this joyful decorating journey, I have one small request.

In the spirit of spreading positivity, it would make my day if you could take just a moment to leave an honest, positive review about your experience with this book. I know, I know - but hear me out!

You see, your feedback holds so much power. Those few minutes sharing your thoughts provide a massive lift to this community.

When you post a positive review, you send the mystical book algorithms important signals that these décor tips are truly helping people design happier homes.

This then gives the book more visibility so that others can also benefit from the dopamine decor knowledge. Your review spreads the happiness bug.

Plus, your unique perspective may give future readers that final nudge of inspiration to take action. Like a décor recommendation from a trusted friend!

Especially for a little indie book like this, reviews help immensely. So if it resonated and brought you value, please give it a boost!

The goal is getting these feel-good decorating concepts out to as many creative spirits as possible. Your review fuels that dream.

So sincerely, thank you for even considering. Now, onward to crafting heartfelt havens!

Enhancing Your Reading with Complementary Visuals

———

While this guide focuses on clearly articulating the philosophies, psychology, and foundational principles behind dopamine decorating through words, I recognize many readers also appreciate accompanying visual examples.

Pictures allow you to vividly envision how these uplifting design concepts might translate into tangible spaces, color palettes, arrangements, and motifs. You conceptualize more fully when absorbing principles both verbally and visually.

That's why I offer access to the Sofia Meri Interior Design Guide. This photo-rich online resource excellently demonstrates visual examples.

With vivid imagery of finished spaces, the guide allows you to illuminate this book in action.

Scan or follow the link below

rebrand.ly/SofiaMeri

Made in the USA
Monee, IL
16 September 2023

42837262R10066